# Understanding Differences

by Brienna Rossiter

FOCUS READERS®

PIONEER

# www.focusreaders.com

Focus Readers is distributed by North Star Editions:
sales@northstareditions.com | 888-417-0195

Produced for Focus Readers by Red Line Editorial.

Photographs ©: Shutterstock Images, cover, 1, 4, 8, 10, 12, 14 (top), 17, 18, 20; iStockphoto, 6, 14 (bottom)

**Library of Congress Cataloging-in-Publication Data**
Library of Congress Cataloging-in-Publication Data is available on the Library of Congress website.

**ISBN**
978-1-64493-812-6 (hardcover)
978-1-64493-814-0 (paperback)
978-1-64493-818-8 (ebook pdf)
978-1-64493-816-4 (hosted ebook)

Printed in the United States of America
Mankato, MN
012021

# About the Author

Brienna Rossiter is a writer and editor who lives in Minnesota. She loves cooking food and being outside.

# Table of Contents

# Chapter 1

# Exploring Differences

The world is home to many, many people. We live in different places. We have many kinds of clothes and food. Our bodies look different, too.

Some people may not talk like you. They may not look like you. They may do things you don't understand. But that doesn't mean they are bad or wrong. It just means you have different ways of living. You can still show **respect** to them.

# Chapter 2

# Appearance and Ability

People's skin comes in many colors. Their bodies have different shapes and sizes. People also have different **abilities**. For example, some people use wheelchairs.

Don't **assume** things about people because of how they look. Instead, get to know them. Remember that each person is **unique**. It is important to treat all people with kindness.

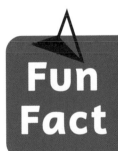

**Fun Fact**

Listening is a great way to learn about other people.

# Chapter 3

# Ideas and Beliefs

People have different **cultures**. They have different **religions**. Culture and religion shape how people live. Examples include the food people eat and the clothes they wear.

People may talk differently from you. They may not act like you do. But don't make fun of them. And don't assume your way of doing things is best. Instead, learn about how other people think and live.

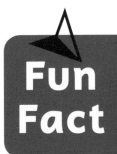

**Fun Fact** People can have many different kinds of families.

# Stop Stereotypes

**Stereotypes** say that everyone in a certain group is alike. These ideas are not true. They are also unkind. Don't repeat them, even as a joke. If other people use a stereotype, speak up. Help them see how their words are hurtful to others.

# Stereotypes Can Be About:

race

culture

ability

gender

# Chapter 4

# Curious and Kind

It's okay to notice the ways people are different. It's also okay to ask questions. Talking helps people understand one another.

However, it's not okay to be rude. Don't point or stare. And don't say mean things. Instead, choose your words carefully. Think of how you might make others feel. Try to make them feel **included** and welcome.

# FOCUS ON
# Understanding Differences

*Write your answers on a separate piece of paper.*

1. Write a sentence explaining what a stereotype is.

2. Have you met someone who wasn't like you? How were you different? What did you have in common?

3. What is a good way to talk about differences?
   A. Make fun of people.
   B. Say mean things.
   C. Ask a question.

4. Why shouldn't you point or stare at other people?
   A. You could hurt their feelings.
   B. You could hurt your arm.
   C. You could change your mind.

*Answer key on page 24.*

# Glossary

**abilities**
Ways that people can use their minds or bodies.

**assume**
To think something without making sure it's correct.

**cultures**
The ways that groups of people live, including their traditions and beliefs.

**included**
Made part of a group.

**religions**
Beliefs about a god or gods, or about how to live a good life.

**respect**
Care for someone's thoughts and feelings.

**stereotypes**
Unfair or untrue ideas about what all members of a certain group are like.

**unique**
Different from everyone or everything else.

# To Learn More

## BOOKS

Herzog, Brad. *W Is for Welcome: A Celebration of America's Diversity.* Ann Arbor, MI: Sleeping Bear Press, 2018.

Krekelberg, Alyssa. *No One Is the Same: Appreciating Differences.* Mankato, MN: The Child's World, 2020.

## NOTE TO EDUCATORS

Visit **www.focusreaders.com** to find lesson plans, activities, links, and other resources related to this title.

# Index

Answer Key: **1.** Answers will vary; **2.** Answers will vary; **3.** C; **4.** A